# Drawing Conclusions

Advanced

## The Jamestown Comprehension Skills Series with Writing Activities

## THIRD EDITION

JAMESTOWN PUBLISHERS

*a division of* NTC/CONTEMPORARY PUBLISHING GROUP
Lincolnwood, Illinois USA

ISBN: 0-8092-0159-3

Published by Jamestown Publishers,
a division of NTC/Contemporary Publishing Group, Inc.
©2000 NTC/Contemporary Publishing Group, Inc.,
4255 West Touhy Avenue, Lincolnwood Illinois 60712-1975 U.S.A.

8 9 10 12 QLM 13 12 11

# INTRODUCTION

The Comprehension Skills Series has been prepared to help students develop specific reading comprehension skills. Each book is completely self-contained. There is no separate answer key or instruction manual. Throughout the book, clear and concise directions guide the student through the lessons and exercises.

The titles of the Comprehension Skills books match the labels found on comprehension questions in other Jamestown textbooks. The student who is having difficulty with a particular kind of question can use the matching Comprehension Skills book for extra instruction and practice to correct the specific weakness.

Each book in the Comprehension Skills Series is divided into five parts.

1. Explanation: Part One (p. 5) clearly defines, explains, and illustrates the specific skill. It begins with a Preview Quiz to get students thinking about the material that will be presented.

2. Instruction: Part Two (p. 7) offers an interesting and informative lesson presented in clear, readable language. This section also utilizes the preview technique introduced in Part One, which requires students to anticipate and respond to the subject matter.

3. Sample Exercise: Part Three (p. 17) consists of a sample exercise with questions. The sample exercise is designed to prepare students for the work required in the following section. Students should read and follow the instructions carefully. When they have finished the exercise, they should read the analysis following it. For each question, there is a step-by-step explanation of why one answer is correct, and why the others are not. Students are urged to consult the teacher if they need extra help before proceeding to Part Four.

**4.** Practice Exercises: Part Four (p. 23) contains twenty practice exercises with questions. Squares (■) bordering the exercises indicate the level of difficulty. The greater the number of squares, the greater the difficulty of the passage. Students are advised to read the instructions and complete the practice exercises thoughtfully and carefully.

**5.** Writing Activities: Part Five (p. 49) contains writing activities that help students apply the skills they have learned in earlier parts of the book. Students should read and follow the instructions carefully. Many activities encourage students to work together cooperatively. The teacher may want to discuss these activities in class.

Each book also contains an Answer Key, which can be found after the Writing Activities. Students can record their scores and monitor their progress on the chart following the Answer Key.

# PART ONE

# *Understanding Conclusions*

**Preview Quiz 1**

As a preview of what will be discussed in Part One, try to answer this question:

**What is a conclusion?**

   a.  a decision about the outcome that certain conditions will produce

   b.  a decision about the cause of a certain outcome

   c.  a decision about the credibility of an argument

Begin reading Part One to discover how conclusions are different from other types of decisions.

    A writer does not always state clearly and directly all the information he or she wishes to communicate. A writer may leave some things unsaid because the writer expects that you, the reader, will draw the proper conclusion on your own. In other cases, things go unsaid because the writer is writing for a purpose somewhat different from the reader's purpose for reading. The writer leaves things unsaid—even though he or she understands them to be true—simply because these things are not specifically pertinent to the writer's purpose in writing. You, the reader, must draw your own conclusions in order to reach an understanding suitable to *your* purposes. This is why you need to know how to draw accurate conclusions when you are reading.

What is a conclusion? A conclusion is a decision about the probable effects of certain conditions. To see what a reasonable and sound conclusion is, first read the following paragraph.

> The drought and heat wave that have plagued western South Dakota show no signs of abating. Forests in the Black Hills are dangerously dry. Record temperatures are likely to continue for at least another week, say long-range forecasters at the National Weather Service. Health officials caution that extreme temperatures make work and exercise much more difficult, especially for older people and people with a history of heart disease.

Based on the information in this paragraph and on general knowledge about weather, fire, and health, a reader can draw several reasonable conclusions.

Because we know that South Dakota has had a drought and that the drought is expected to continue, we can conclude that people in the area should not waste water.

From the fact that forests in the Black Hills are dangerously dry, we can conclude that campers in the Black Hills should use extreme caution with campfires.

The paragraph points out the dangers of extreme temperatures, especially for older people and people with a history of heart disease. It also states that high temperatures are likely to continue for a week. From that information, we can conclude that older people and people with a history of heart disease should avoid unnecessary exercise during the coming week.

Each of these is a reasonable conclusion based on general knowledge and on the information in the paragraph.

# PART TWO

# Drawing a Conclusion

## Preview Quiz 2

As a preview of what will be discussed next, try to answer this question:

**What is a cause-and-effect relationship?**

a. a relationship in which it is impossible to decide why events occur

b. a relationship that cannot be described accurately

c. a relationship in which one event makes another happen

Continue reading to discover the correct answer.

The first step in drawing a conclusion is to recognize potential cause-and-effect relationships in what you read. A great deal of logical thinking is based on cause-and-effect relationships. We know from experience that certain events cause other events, that certain causes imply certain effects. A rainstorm wets the pavement. The rainstorm is the cause; wet pavement is the effect. Wet pavement makes automobile tires slip. This time, wet pavement is the cause; tires slipping is the effect. Falling rain implies wet pavement, and wet pavement implies slippery conditions.

There are other ways to state these cause-and-effect relationships. A writer expressing them might do so in any of the following ways:

> Because rain is falling, the pavement will get wet.
> Rain is falling; therefore, the pavement will get wet.
>
> Since the pavement is wet, the tires will slip.
> The pavement is wet, so the tires will slip.

Often, however, writers omit the effects. They state the cause, but merely imply the effect. Therefore, your first step in drawing a conclusion is to decide which statements imply certain results. Consider the statements in the following paragraph:

> Why do some birds migrate while others stay at home all winter? Most birds that migrate do so not because they dislike cold weather but because food is harder to find in cold weather. Seeds are available year-round, but many insects hibernate during winter. One American bird, the dickcissel of the Midwest, a member of the finch family, is an eater of grasshoppers and locusts. It winters in Central and South America. In contrast, the house sparrow, another member of the finch family, is a seedeater with a short, sturdy bill that is ideally suited to cracking seeds.

Notice some facts that imply certain outcomes:

> Seeds are available year-round . . .
> Many insects hibernate during winter . . .
> The house sparrow . . . is a seedeater . . .

These are causes, but the writer has left their effects unstated. From the information in the rest of the paragraph, we can see certain effects that these causes imply:

Seeds are available year-round, so **birds that eat seeds do not have to migrate.**

Many insects hibernate during winter; therefore, **birds that eat insects must travel to warmer climates where insects are active.**

Because the house sparrow is a seedeater, **the house sparrow does not have to migrate.**

**Preview Quiz 3**

As a preview of what will be discussed next, try to answer this question:

*Why is it important to consider all the implications of what you read?*

   a.  because each cause can result in one and only one effect

   b.  because one set of facts may lead to several conclusions

   c.  because most causes have no effect whatsoever

Continue reading to discover the correct answer.

A single cause may produce several effects. Therefore, one set of facts may lead to several conclusions. Because this is so, it is important to consider a range of possible effects before settling on a conclusion. This raises an important point about reading: good readers are actively engaged with the material they are reading, always thinking about it, considering it, weighing it, trying to decide where it leads, what it suggests, and what it implies. Good readers keep an open mind and do not jump to conclusions. Instead, they stretch their thinking and consider all the implications before settling on the most likely conclusion or conclusions.

To see how important it is to consider all the implications, read the paragraph on the next page, which outlines some of the events leading to World War I. As you read, pay particular attention to potential cause-and-effect relationships.

By 1908 tension in Europe was becoming alarming.
The French were firmly opposed to Germany, which
had annexed Alsace and part of Lorraine after the
Franco-Prussian War. Serbia and Russia supported
the efforts of Slavs to break free from the
Austro-Hungarian Empire and create a Slavic nation.
Germany was expanding its empire in the Middle
East, where Great Britain had long-standing interests.
Earlier, Germany had formed an alliance with Russia
and Austria-Hungary, but in 1871 Germany turned
from Russia and formed a Dual Alliance with
Austria-Hungary alone; later Italy joined them.
France needed allies to oppose this formidable Triple
Alliance.

Many statements in the paragraph are causes that imply
certain effects. Following are some of them, with the word
*because* added to each to indicate that it is a potential cause:

> **Because** Serbia and Russia supported the efforts of
> Slavs to break free from the Austro-Hungarian
> Empire . . .

> **Because** Germany was expanding its empire in the
> Middle East, where Great Britain had long-standing
> interests . . .

> **Because** Germany turned from Russia and formed a
> Dual Alliance with Austria-Hungary alone . . .

> **Because** France needed allies to oppose this
> formidable Triple Alliance . . .

What effects do these causes imply? Try to think of as many
as you can. Review the paragraph. Brainstorm. Jot down a
list of potential effects; you will evaluate them in the next
section.

────── **Preview Quiz 4** ──────

As a preview of what will be discussed next, try to answer this question:

*Within a paragraph, how are the causes and effects likely to be related?*

   a. They will not be related.

   b. Each cause-and-effect relationship will be separate from any of the others.

   c. They will be interrelated.

Continue reading to discover the correct answer.

Because most writing is organized by topic, theme, and idea, you are likely to find that there is a network of causes and effects, not just a simple straight line. When you see the interrelationships of these causes and effects, you may see how they lead to an overall conclusion. At the end of the last section, you listed possible effects of causes mentioned in a paragraph about World War I. Your list of possible effects may have included these:

> **Because** Serbia and Russia supported the efforts of Slavs to break free from the Austro-Hungarian Empire . . .
>
>    Austria-Hungary opposed Serbia.
>    Austria-Hungary opposed Russia.
>    Slavs in Austria-Hungary supported Serbia.
>    Slavs in Austria-Hungary supported Russia.

**Because** Germany was expanding its empire in the Middle East, where Great Britain had long-standing interests . . .
  Great Britain opposed Germany.
  Middle Eastern countries opposed Germany.

**Because** Germany turned from Russia and formed a Dual Alliance with Austria-Hungary alone . . .
  Russia opposed Germany.
  Russia opposed Austria-Hungary.

As you consider these effects, you should begin to see a pattern emerging. Germany, Austria-Hungary, and Italy are allied in the Triple Alliance. For one reason or another, Russia, Great Britain, and Serbia are on bad terms with one or more of the members of the Triple Alliance.

Now let's consider what the final sentence of the paragraph implies:

**Because** France needed allies to oppose this formidable Triple Alliance . . .

In light of the implications earlier in the paragraph, you might conclude that

France turned to Great Britain, Russia, or Serbia.

You would be correct. In fact, France turned to Russia and Great Britain, forming the Triple Entente with them, in opposition to the Triple Alliance. And what about Serbia? World War I began when Archduke Francis Ferdinand of Austria-Hungary was assassinated by a Serbian nationalist. That should not seem surprising if you read the paragraph carefully and think about all the implications of the statements in it.

From your work with this paragraph, you should see that it is important to consider all the implications of the statements in a piece of writing before you draw a conclusion. Keep an open mind; consider all the possibilities.

---

**Preview Quiz 5**

As a preview of what will be discussed next, try to answer this question:

***What is the ultimate test of a reasonable conclusion?***

    a. Does it conform to the rules of the formal logical syllogism?

    b. Does it make sense?

    c. Does it match the writer's conclusions?

Continue reading to discover the correct answer.

---

Sometimes it is necessary to draw a conclusion not from a direct statement in a piece of writing but from the unstated main idea of the writing. Consider the information in this paragraph:

> The cactus plant usually has a thick green trunk. This trunk performs the photosynthesis that, in other plants, is performed by leaves. Generally, cactus plants do not have leaves. The leaves of a tree expose an enormous surface area to the sun and wind. All over that surface area evaporation of water takes place continuously. The trunk of the cactus, in contrast, exposes a much smaller area, thereby reducing evaporation even in the harsh conditions of the desert.

The main idea of the paragraph is not stated, but it is easy to determine. It could be stated as

The cactus plant is well suited to its desert environment.

This fact has several implications that could lead to valid conclusions. You could conclude that if you intend to keep a cactus as a houseplant, you will have to try to duplicate its desert environment. You will have to keep it in a sunny spot, and you will have to be careful not to give it too much water. You can also conclude that, if you live in a desert area, you should forget about planting trees in your yard. From the information in the paragraph and the unstated main idea, you can conclude that trees are not well adapted to a desert environment. Water will evaporate from their leaves too quickly, and they will wither and die.

As you read, watch for potential causes. Think about their implications. Stretch your thinking; go beyond the obvious and try to imagine what all the implications of the statements may be. Remember that one cause may have many effects and one set of facts may lead to several conclusions. Avoid drawing a final conclusion until you are satisfied that you have explored all the avenues that the implications may lead you to. Then put the results of your thinking together. Evaluate them in light of what the writing says and what you know. Decide which outcomes seem most likely. Then draw your conclusions. Test them by deciding whether they make sense; remember that making sense is the ultimate test of any conclusion.

# PART THREE

## Sample Exercise

The exercise on the next page is a sample exercise. Its purpose is to show how the information you have studied in Parts One and Two can be put to use in reading.

A second purpose of the sample exercise is to preview the twenty exercises that appear in Part Four. Reading the sample passage and answering the sample questions will help you get off to a good start.

The answers to all the questions are fully explained. Reasons are given showing why the correct answers are the best answers and where the wrong answers are faulty. In addition, the text describes the thinking you might do as you work through the exercise correctly.

Complete the sample exercise carefully and thoughtfully. Do not go on to Part Four until you are certain that you understand what a conclusion is and how to draw accurate conclusions.

---

## Sample Exercise

Picture yourself, if you will, having to deal with this problem. Rick Donner, a scuba diver, was diving alone in the Pacific off the California coast. His marker buoy, floating on the surface, carried the divers' flag to warn boats that there was a diver down. He had been swimming for an hour, enjoying the solitude among the thick graceful strands of an undersea kelp forest, checking his air supply every so often until, all too soon, it was time to surface. As Rick went up, a huge wave surged past overhead and rolled on toward the shore. At the same time, Rick felt himself jerked backward. The wave had dragged the anchor of his marker buoy, tangling its line around Rick's air hose and tearing it apart. Something had to be done, and quickly.

---

**1.** Because Rick was diving alone, you can conclude that
  a. no one was available to help him.
  b. the warning buoy did not work properly.
  c. he would have to surface sooner.
  d. someone else would soon be swimming by.

**2.** From the fact that the air hose was torn, you can conclude that
  a. another wave was on its way.
  b. air bubbles would alert rescuers.
  c. Rick's air supply would run out soon.
  d. Rick's diving partner would come to his aid.

**3.** From the main idea of the paragraph, you can conclude that a scuba diver
  a. does not require great strength.
  b. should never dive alone.
  c. should avoid swimming in kelp forests.
  d. should not buy used equipment.

**4.** Underline the sentence that supports the conclusion that boats will steer clear of the area where Rick is diving.

# Answers and Explanations

**1.** To complete this sentence, you must decide what conclusion is implied by the fact that Rick was diving alone. Read each possible conclusion and decide whether it is implied by Rick's swimming alone. The best answer is *a.* You can verify this for yourself by thinking of a sentence that states the cause-and-effect relationship: *Because* Rick was diving alone, no one was available to help him.

Answers *b* and *c* are incorrect because both state results that would not be caused by diving alone. The buoy would not be affected by the number of divers, nor would the length of time that Rick could stay below.

Answer *d* is incorrect because it contradicts good sense. If someone is swimming alone, it is *unlikely* that someone else will soon be swimming by.

**2.** Again, completing this sentence requires you to find a
conclusion implied by a cause. In this case, the cause is the
fact that the air hose was torn. In your mind, construct a
sentence in which the cause begins with *because*. Then look
for the best ending to it. The best answer is *c: Because* the
air hose was torn, Rick's air supply would run out soon.
This is a reasonable conclusion.

Answer *a* is incorrect because the coming of another
wave would not be affected by a torn air hose; there is
no relationship between the two events.

Answer *b* is incorrect because air bubbles could only
alert rescuers if there were any nearby; we know from
other evidence in the paragraph that there were none.

Answer *d* is incorrect because we know that Rick was
diving alone; he had no diving partner.

**3.** To complete this sentence, you must first decide what the main idea of the paragraph is. The story seems to lead to the idea that because of the possibility of the kind of trouble Rick got into, a diver should never dive alone. The best answer is *b*.

Answer *a* is incorrect because nothing in the paragraph implies that strength is not needed. In fact, Rick might have been able to resist the force of the wave if he were stronger.

Answer *c* is incorrect because there is no relationship between Rick's swimming in the kelp forest and the wave; the wave caused the trouble, not the kelp.

Answer *d* is incorrect because it is not at all relevant to the facts in the paragraph. Nothing is mentioned about used equipment. Perhaps buying used equipment is not a good idea, but nothing in this paragraph leads to that conclusion.

**4.** When you are told to find a sentence that supports a certain conclusion, you are being told to find the cause of a certain effect. To do so, review the paragraph to find a likely cause, and then test it by adding the word *because* to it and seeing whether it implies the effect. The best answer is the sentence "His marker buoy, floating on the surface, carried the divers' flag to warn boats that there was a diver down." Try the test: *Because* his marker buoy, floating on the surface, carried the divers' flag to warn boats that there was a diver down, boats would steer clear of the area.

If you had difficulty answering these questions correctly, review the paragraph and questions. If, after that, you still do not understand the answers and explanations, check with your instructor before going on.

# PART FOUR

## *Practice Exercises*

- The twenty exercises that follow are designed to help you put to use your ability to understand conclusions and draw accurate conclusions.

- Each exercise is just like the sample exercise you completed in Part Three.

- Read each passage well. Answer the questions carefully and thoughtfully.

- Correct your answers using the Answer Key at the back of the book. Mark your scores on the chart on page 64 before going on to the next exercise.

## Practice Exercise *1*

Before the development of modern printing methods, most paper was made of flax and hemp, the same fibers that were used to make cloth. When cheap, high-speed printing arrived, the demand for books skyrocketed. Paper manufacturers shifted from flax and hemp to wood, which was in much greater supply. Today, most paper is made from wood, and therein lies a problem. The most widely used method of turning wood into paper uses acids, and this produces paper high in acid content. Over time, the acids react with air, moisture, and sunlight and make the paper brittle. It becomes so brittle that it cracks, crumbles, and even falls into dust. Paper with a high "rag content"—that is, paper made literally from rags or from fibers more like flax and hemp—is not subject to the same decaying process.

1. Because the demand for books suddenly increased when cheap, high-speed printing arrived, you can conclude that
   a. paper manufacturers were forced out of business.
   b. books had to be made to last longer.
   c. writers made much more money then than now.
   d. paper manufacturers had to increase production.

2. From the fact that paper made from wood becomes so brittle that it falls into dust, you can conclude that
   a. some books simply fall apart after a while.
   b. paper manufacturers are cheating the public.
   c. wood is dangerous as a building material.
   d. paper manufacturers had to increase production.

3. From the main idea of the paragraph, you can conclude that
   a. flax makes fine, durable fabrics for clothing.
   b. hemp makes flexible, durable rope.
   c. paper manufacturers use acids unnecessarily.
   d. many books may be in danger of falling apart.

4. Underline the sentence that supports the conclusion that paper with high rag content is best for long-lasting books.

## — Practice Exercise **2** —

The male and female mosquito make an odd couple. The female is a vampire that lives on blood and may even need blood for the proper development of her eggs. The male is a vegetarian that sips nectar and plant juices. Females of different species choose different hosts on which to dine. Some feed exclusively on cattle, horses, birds, and other warm-blooded creatures. Some favor cold-blooded animals. Still others prefer human beings.

While the female's menu varies, her bite remains the same. She drives her sharp, tubular snout through the skin and injects a fluid to keep the blood from clotting. Then she drinks her fill of the freely flowing blood. The fluid that she injects may carry disease germs if she has previously bitten a diseased animal. After her blood meal, she rests while her eggs develop. She then looks for standing water in which to lay her eggs—a pond, a pool, a swamp, or even a pail of rainwater.

**1.** From information in the paragraphs, you can conclude that a mosquito that bites you at a picnic is
a. male.      b. diseased.      c. female.      d. resting.

**2.** From the fact that the fluid that a mosquito injects may carry disease germs, you can conclude that mosquitoes
a. are a health hazard to most living creatures.
b. cannot be controlled effectively.
c. render important services to humankind.
d. are a necessary element in the balance of nature.

**3.** Because the injected fluid keeps blood from clotting,
a. the victim may become diseased.
b. the mosquito's eggs develop.
c. the blood flows freely.
d. it may contain germs.

**4.** Underline the sentence that implies that it would be wise to empty a wading pool during mosquito breeding season.

## Practice Exercise 3

To be completely accurate, the word *duck* should be used only for the female members of the bird family *Anatidae* (UH-nad-uhdee). The males are called *drakes*. However, in popular usage *duck* applies to the whole family. Ducks protect themselves from cold water by waterproofing themselves. Like most birds, ducks have glands that secrete oils. They use their bills to rub the waxy oil over their feathers. Under the oiled feathers is a layer of smaller, soft feathers called *down*. Down keeps ducks warm by trapping air under the outside feathers. Ducks that feed on the surface have light, hollow bones. Mergansers and other diving ducks have heavier bones than surface-feeding ducks. Diving ducks are excellent swimmers.

Most drakes are more brightly colored than female ducks. However, at the end of the mating season most ducks molt; that is, they lose their feathers. When they molt they are unable to fly. The drakes lose their brilliant plumage and turn a drabber but safer brown, like that of the females.

1. You can conclude that diving ducks are heavier than surface ducks because
    a. they eat more food.
    b. they survive only in cold climates.
    c. they do not lose their bright plumage after mating.
    d. their weight helps them stay underwater.

2. From the fact that the diving ducks are excellent underwater swimmers, you can conclude that
    a. other ducks cannot swim underwater.
    b. diving ducks are able to pursue fish underwater.
    c. diving ducks do not molt.
    d. diving ducks do not require protective coloration.

3. For a while after the mating season is over, drakes
    a. do not swim.
    b. are unable to secrete oils normally.
    c. are more vulnerable than usual.
    d. acquire bright, brilliantly colored plumage.

4. Underline the sentence that supports the conclusion in number 3.

Practice Exercise 4

One thing strikes a visitor at Walnut Hills Community Elementary School near Denver. The rooms are gigantic and *there aren't any desks.* But watch your step! Children are lying all over the floor, some reading by themselves, some doing worksheets in groups of twos and threes, and others sitting in small groups asking questions of an adult. It looks as if the children have rebelled, occupied the superintendent's office, and are running the school the way they would like. But the superintendent of the Cherry Creek School District knows the school is running just the way he likes it. Many of the children come to school early and leave late—by choice. Absences have been halved. What's more, the children are learning academic subjects far better than average. And they understand a lot more about themselves and others than most children do.

**1.** From the fact that many of the children choose to come to school early and leave late, you can conclude that
   a. they enjoy the atmosphere at Walnut Hills.
   b. children are unpredictable.
   c. educators at Walnut Hills are discouraged.
   d. classrooms are poorly furnished.

**2.** From the fact that the children are learning academic subjects far better than average, you can conclude that
   a. the educators at Walnut Hills are discouraged.
   b. the techniques described are educationally sound.
   c. the superintendent is likely to be fired.
   d. there is a serious lack of equipment in the district.

**3.** Educators at the Walnut Hills Community Elementary School are
   a. misguided.
   b. uninterested.
   c. creative.
   d. traditional.

**4.** Underline the sentence that supports the conclusion that changes at Walnut Hills have improved attendance.

---- Practice Exercise **5** ----

In recent years, millions of Americans have embraced the bicycle as if it were a startling new invention. There are more than seventy million bikes in the United States today, more than two for every three automobiles. Of course, the bike has been around for more than 160 years, and this isn't America's first bicycle boom. A wave of bike enthusiasm swept the land in the late 1800s, and bicycle production hit two million units in 1897. Then, with the coming of the auto, bicycling declined, and for decades it remained popular only with children and a few adult faddists. Now, a national preoccupation with air pollution and physical fitness has brought the bike back to the forefront. In a recent year, more than eight million bikes were sold in the United States, and a third of them went to adults. The year before, only 15 percent of new bike sales were for adults.

**1.** From the fact that it has been around for 160 years, you can conclude that the bicycle is likely to
a. be abandoned soon.
b. disappear when a replacement for the car is found.
c. endure through waves of enthusiasm and neglect.
d. reach record sales in the coming year.

**2.** From the main idea of the paragraph, you can conclude that the bicycle is
a. enjoying a strong revival.　　c. popular only with children.
b. creating traffic problems.　　d. replacing the family car.

**3.** You can conclude that
a. bicycle sales to adults are growing especially fast.
b. more than ten million bikes will be sold next year.
c. 40 percent of sales will be to adults next year.
d. children are losing interest in bicycling.

**4.** Underline the two sentences that support the correct answer for number 3.

— Practice Exercise **6** —

November 9, 1965—it was a pleasant day. The evening exodus from the hearts of the great cities had just begun, when, without warning, lights in office towers flickered out and died at 5:16 p.m. Thousands of feet above, astonished airline pilots saw Manhattan fade, then disappear. In eight minutes, a near total electrical eclipse had swept over an area slightly smaller than Great Britain but crowded with thirty million people. A massive power failure had torn the intricate electrical grid that served parts of eight states and sections of Ontario, Canada. The Great Blackout, as it came to be called, was the first dramatic warning that the relationship between energy supply and demand had reached a precarious balance.

**1.** From the fact that all electrical power was lost in the affected area, you can conclude that
   a. elevators stopped.
   b. traffic lights blinked out.
   c. subway trains ground to a halt.
   d. all of the above occurred.

**2.** Because an electrical failure could sweep through such a large area in eight minutes, you can conclude that
   a. such a thing could never happen again.
   b. the distribution network was fragile.
   c. Great Britain is likely to suffer a similar outage since it is approximately the same size.
   d. high demand in Manhattan was the cause.

**3.** You can conclude that
   a. planes en route to Manhattan had to land elsewhere.
   b. people in Great Britain began to panic when they heard the news.
   c. Canadians later withdrew from the electrical grid.
   d. people in the area sold their homes and moved.

**4.** Underline the sentence that supports the conclusion in number 3.

## Practice Exercise 7

Shy, wary, and seldom seen, perhaps no creature in nature has suffered so much as the wise, perceptive raven. It is a shiny black bird, a member of the crow family. Primarily a scavenger, it will, like the other members of the crow family, eat grain crops, eggs, and fledgling chicks. Its call is a harsh, croaking caw. It can be tamed and taught to perform complicated tricks, even to mimic human speech.

The raven has been the object of superstition for centuries. In the myths and folklore of many countries, the raven was a bird of evil. Even the mere sighting of a raven was believed an evil omen. If one alighted on a church or dwelling, it was taken as a certain sign of death or disaster. In certain areas of the United States, some people still believe that the raven is an evil omen.

1. Because the raven sometimes eats crops, eggs, and chicks, you can conclude that
   a. farmers are fond of the magnificent bird.
   b. farmers dislike the bird.
   c. eggs make a bird's coat shiny.
   d. it is an intelligent bird.

2. From the fact that the raven's call is a harsh, croaking caw, you can conclude that
   a. its call does not win it friends and admirers.
   b. many people love to listen to it sing.
   c. it is possessed by demons.
   d. it is a shy, cautious bird.

3. From the main idea, you can conclude that the
   a. raven is an evil bird.
   b. raven is a friend to farmers everywhere, celebrated in the folklore of many countries.
   c. raven is an endangered species.
   d. raven's appearance, call, and habits inspired superstitions about it.

4. Underline the sentence that supports the conclusion that the raven is an intelligent bird.

## Practice Exercise 8

Freeways and streets often begin their careers with extra-wide lines. But soon traffic becomes heavier, and pressure increases on highway officials to "do something" about the congestion. Adding new lanes will require heavy equipment to create a base for a new road, perhaps digging away a hillside or widening a bridge. And it will take time. Officials may compromise and add part of a lane to the shoulder, move the paint stripes over a few inches, and create four lanes where three had been. It requires no heavy equipment and it's quick. Unfortunately, narrow lanes mean less room for drivers to correct their mistakes or inattention, and less room for the swaying of a car in a crosswind. Two cars on narrow lanes may actually touch even though the tires will be within their respective lanes.

1. Because adding new lanes will require heavy equipment and a great deal of work, you can conclude that doing so is
   a. the best solution.          c. expensive.
   b. the traditional solution.   d. inexpensive.

2. Because moving paint stripes requires no heavy equipment, you can conclude that doing so is
   a. the best solution.          c. expensive.
   b. the traditional solution.   d. inexpensive.

3. From the main idea, you can conclude that increasing the capacity of a road by narrowing the lanes
   a. is a costly, difficult, and time-consuming process.
   b. leads to safer, less congested roads.
   c. offers the best long-term solution to congestion.
   d. is quick and cheap but potentially dangerous.

4. Underline the sentences that allow you to conclude that narrow lanes increase the danger of sideswipe collisions.

— Practice Exercise **9** —

Most of us are reluctant to accept the fact that our natural resources are fixed—have been fixed, in fact, since Earth was created. We want to go on using virgin materials. We aren't educated to reusing resources, or even recognizing the value of "waste" products. Currently, we are fearful of losing the use of our water and air to pollution. Perhaps, in the end, this fear may prove to be a good thing. We once thought of water and air as free, but they are not, not any more than the land is free. People haven't wanted to be educated about the part they must play in solving our environmental problems.

**1.** The main idea leads to the conclusion that
   a. our attitudes lead to waste and pollution.
   b. virgin materials are superior to recycled products.
   c. we must adjust to shortages and high prices.
   d. we can clean up our rivers and lakes.

**2.** Which sentence states the reasoning that led the writer to conclude that "this fear may prove to be a good thing"?
   a. Because we fear air and water pollution, we will lapse into an era of pessimism and decay.
   b. Because we fear air and water pollution, we will change our thinking about reusing resources.
   c. Because we fear government controls, we will find better ways to dispose of waste.
   d. Because we fear recycled materials, we will find new ways to exploit dwindling resources.

**3.** If it is true that as a group "we want to go on using virgin materials," then we will
   a. enact legislation to that effect.
   b. eliminate pollution by using them.
   c. eliminate the fear we now feel.
   d. exhaust a fixed supply of resources.

**4.** Underline the sentence that supports the conclusion that we now discard products that are potentially useful.

_____ Practice Exercise **10** _____

All the guns around me now are in the hands of prison guards, but for fifteen years the guns were in my hands. Guns were my life, and your pharmacy was my business. I was a professional bandit, and among the places I robbed over the years I can count more than forty drugstores.

Why did I choose drugstores over other targets? I'll tell you, and I hope it will serve as a warning to the people who own and operate them. Most druggists simply don't believe holdups are ever going to happen to them. Most drugstores are located in areas where pedestrian traffic is heavy. There are narcotics on the premises. Pharmacies, moreover, are seldom heavily staffed.

**1.** Because most druggists don't believe that they will be held up, you can conclude that they
   a. take steps to protect their stores.
   b. are lax about security.
   c. close in the evening.
   d. demand police protection.

**2.** Because most drugstores are located in areas where pedestrian traffic is heavy,
   a. a thief can get "lost in the crowd."
   b. they are not attractive targets for thieves.
   c. they are difficult to find.
   d. they go unnoticed by the police.

**3.** Because narcotics are kept on the premises in drugstores, you can conclude that
   a. most people avoid entering drugstores.
   b. police avoid patrolling near drugstores.
   c. thieves do not consider drugstores worth robbing.
   d. thieves who are addicts are attracted to drugstores.

**4.** Underline the sentence that allows you to conclude that a thief usually finds little opposition in a drugstore.

— Practice Exercise *11* ————————————

A purebred dog is a type of dog that is recognized by the American Kennel Club as a distinct breed. When they are mature, purebred dogs of the same breed vary little in size, weight, and other physical traits. In addition, dogs of a particular breed usually have definite temperament and behavior characteristics.

On the other hand, mongrels, or dogs of mixed breeds, vary widely and unpredictably. The cute, cuddly, mongrel puppy that you select at random may grow into a big, long-haired, pony-sized animal instead of the small pet you really wanted. The long-legged mongrel puppy that you visualize as a large-sized companion for country walks may stop growing soon and turn out to be a small, house-loving pet.

1. From the information in the first paragraph, you can conclude that if you buy a purebred puppy
   a. it will be of moderate size when it is grown.
   b. it will be more attractive than a mongrel dog.
   c. you can predict its characteristics when it is grown.
   d. you will have a large-sized companion for country walks.

2. From the information in the second paragraph, you can conclude that if you buy a mongrel puppy
   a. it will be of moderate size when it is grown.
   b. it will be more attractive than a purebred dog.
   c. you cannot predict its characteristics when it is grown.
   d. you will have a large-sized companion for country walks.

3. From the main idea, you can conclude that the greatest advantage in choosing a purebred puppy is that it is
   a. predictable.          c. superior.
   b. adaptable.           d. inferior.

4. Underline the sentence that supports the conclusion that purebred dogs enjoy a definite status.

## ── Practice Exercise *12* ──

Most of the huge presses that are used to make objects from sheets of metal are driven by hydraulic pressure, and therefore they are called hydraulic presses. Basically, a hydraulic press has three parts: a small cylinder with a small piston inside it, a large cylinder with a large piston inside it, and a pipe that connects the two cylinders. The whole device is filled with fluid. When a force is applied to the small piston, the fluid transmits the force to the large piston. The small piston is pushed with a small force through a long distance, and the large piston moves through a short distance with a much greater force. This large piston presses the sheet of metal against the die that shapes it.

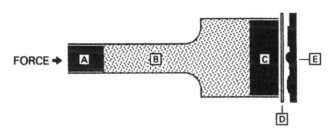

1. From the information in the passage, you can conclude that part A in the diagram is the
   a. fluid.                  c. large cylinder.
   b. small piston.           d. sheet metal.

2. From the information in the passage, you can conclude that part B in the diagram is the
   a. die.                    c. small piston.
   b. large piston.           d. fluid.

3. From the information in the passage, you can conclude that part D in the diagram is the
   a. die.                    c. large piston.
   b. small piston.           d. sheet metal.

4. Underline the sentence that allows you to reach a conclusion about the part labeled E in the diagram.

## Practice Exercise *13*

How do you reach and inspire youngsters who have turned off and given up on furthering their education? How do you convince them that regular attendance at high school courses will eventually provide them with the tools for success? Edward F. Carpenter, headmaster of "The Prep," as it is known by the students, admits that it isn't easy. "We reach these young people with the concept of school as a place where they will find respect, belief in their abilities, and an attitude of sincerely caring about their problems," Carpenter states. "Our purpose is to build within the students an awareness of their worth and capabilities and to persuade them that there is a group of adults as well as members of their own peer group who will pull with them."

1. From the statements that headmaster Carpenter makes, you can conclude that "The Prep" works at
   a. improving the self-image of young people.
   b. protecting youthful offenders from prosecution.
   c. maintaining law and order in the streets.
   d. transforming athletes into students.

2. You can conclude that headmaster Carpenter
   a. teaches English.
   b. considers traditional academic subjects of primary importance.
   c. considers attitudes as important as academics.
   d. uses sports to build character.

3. You can conclude that headmaster Carpenter thinks "turned-off" youngsters respond to
   a. traditional education.
   b. formal discipline.
   c. financial incentive.
   d. individualized attention.

4. Underline the sentence that supports the conclusion that headmaster Carpenter does not have any illusions about the difficulty of his job.

## Practice Exercise 14

In the minds of many Americans, Boston is a kind of historic blur, a vast urban museum of old monuments, baked bean factories, and people named Lowell and Cabot who talk only to each other and to God. The musty aura of Boston's image may linger in part because the city itself doesn't boast of being the biggest or boomingest of places, nor does it aspire to such goals. In its own low-key self-promotion, Boston neither brags of its past nor projects some galactic future. Boston prides itself on being *livable*. It is not just old monuments or just contemporary dazzle, but a growing variety of attractions that has made Boston seem so livable. This perception of the city is so widespread that, a few years ago, in a survey of Ivy League graduates, Boston replaced New York as the city most favored as a place to live and work after college.

**1.** The paragraph supports the conclusion that a livable city
   a. is brassy and booming.
   b. projects a galactic future.
   c. avoids extremes.
   d. follows tradition.

**2.** From the description in the paragraph, you can conclude that the people of Boston
   a. have a sense of history and a view of the future.
   b. are self-centered and ignore the rest of the country.
   c. are dull and old-fashioned.
   d. have no drive and ambition.

**3.** If Boston is a kind of historic blur in the minds of many Americans, then they are
   a. correct.
   b. incorrect.
   c. interested in history.
   d. Ivy League graduates.

**4.** Underline the sentence that supports the conclusion in number 1.

— Practice Exercise **15** —

"Buckle up . . . or else!" may become the slogan of those who support safety belts. Studies have shown that most injuries and deaths resulting from accidents are caused when people are thrown out of or against the interior of the vehicle. Forty-five percent of those killed in auto accidents would have been saved if they had been wearing safety belts. Safety belts have been standard equipment on all automobiles sold in the United States for more than thirty years. Since long before that, safety-minded organizations have been advocating that motor vehicle drivers and passengers make it a habit to use safety belts whether they are driving across the country or across town. Millions of dollars worth of public service advertising has been donated by newspapers, magazines, radio, and television to remind motorists and passengers to "buckle up."

1. Since most injuries are caused by being thrown out of or against the interior of the vehicle, you can conclude that
   a. people are better off if they can leap out of a car.
   b. people are better off if they are strapped in place.
   c. safety belts themselves must be causing injuries.
   d. most people must be using safety belts.

2. Because 45 percent of those killed in auto accidents were not wearing safety belts, you can conclude that
   a. nearly everyone wears safety belts now.
   b. only careless drivers do not wear safety belts.
   c. the cost of installing safety belts has been wasted.
   d. many people do not wear safety belts.

3. The campaign for safety belts is supported by
   a. insurance companies only.
   b. all licensed motorists.
   c. safety organizations only.
   d. safety organizations and the media.

4. Underline the sentence that supports the conclusion that the lifesaving value of safety belts has been established.

## Practice Exercise *16*

Coleridge's "Ancient Mariner," becalmed upon a glassy ocean and dying of thirst, was not the only one to be surrounded by water he dared not drink. Our rivers and lakes are in serious trouble as they continue to bear never-intended burdens of pollution and industrial expansion. Our waters are not fit to drink unless they are first treated or purified. At a treatment station, water may pass through several processes. Filtration is the simplest and most obvious of these; the water is passed through filters, which may be fine or coarse, depending on how the water will be used. Next, the water may be aerated—sprayed into the air to release gases dissolved in it. Bacteria in water can be eliminated by adding chlorine, bubbling ozone through the water, or exposing the water to ultraviolet light. All of these treatment methods are expensive. Treating our waste water *before* it is discharged into lakes, rivers, or the ocean is far less expensive.

**1.** You can conclude that filtration removes
a. gases.
b. bacteria.
c. dirt.
d. ozone.

**2.** You can conclude that at a treatment station what looks like a fountain is
a. an aeration device.
b. a monument to Coleridge.
c. intended to heighten community awareness.
d. meant to emphasize recreational uses of water.

**3.** It is logical to conclude that chlorine, ozone, and ultraviolet light
a. are cheap methods of treating water.
b. release gases trapped in water.
c. are troublesome pollutants in water.
d. will kill bacteria.

**4.** Underline the sentence that supports the conclusion that sewage treatment is the first step in water treatment.

---

## Practice Exercise 17

The magic spades of archaeology have given us the whole lost world of Egypt. Thanks to the Egyptian climate, we know more about the vanished Egyptians than we know about any other ancient people, much more than we know about the early Greeks and Romans, whose civilizations died just yesterday. The climate in Egypt is extremely dry. Almost nothing rots, spoils, or crumbles away. Dig up the most delicate carving, the finest substance, and you will find it as fresh and perfect after thousands of years of lying in the sand as if it had recently come from the artist's hand. The Egyptians often buried useful objects with their dead. When they didn't bury the actual objects, they buried little models of them, exact reproductions of the real things. Is it any wonder that we have a complete record of their civilization?

---

1. Because the climate in Egypt is extremely dry,
   a. ancient civilizations are not buried very deep.
   b. archaeologists must use advanced digging methods.
   c. almost nothing rots, spoils, or crumbles away.
   d. the Egyptians had to use secret methods of preservation.

2. From the fact that Egyptians often buried useful objects with their dead, you can conclude that the Egyptians
   a. were advanced in the arts.
   b. thought the dead needed these things.
   c. had no respect for their dead.
   d. were interested in archaeology.

3. Because the Egyptians buried useful objects or models of them with their dead,
   a. archaeology is more widely respected.
   b. we know what objects the Egyptians used.
   c. Egyptian civilization was a model for the Greeks.
   d. they have crumbled to dust.

4. Underline the sentence that supports the conclusion that the climate in Greece and Rome does not preserve artifacts as well as the Egyptian climate does.

## — Practice Exercise 18 —

Scientists are studying causes and cures for the peculiar malady known as "jet lag." Our bodies are programmed for rhythmic changes during each twenty-four-hour period called the "circadian cycle," generating more energy during daytime hours, less at night, and so on. When we hop a jet and fly through six time zones, our system gets confused, and we may spend the first days of that vacation feeling exhausted because our bodies don't know what time it is. You can lessen the shock of change by following these steps:

- Start adjusting to your new time schedule a few days before beginning your trip.
- Get as much sleep as possible en route to your destination.
- Break long trips with stopovers. Upon arrival, take it easy. Don't try to adjust to local time schedules all at once.

**1.** If you start adjusting to your new time schedule a few days before beginning your trip, then you will
a. have a smaller adjustment to make on arrival.
b. be exhausted by the time you arrive.
c. cross fewer time zones during your trip.
d. better understand the "circadian cycle."

**2.** If you get as much sleep as possible en route to your destination, then you will
a. trick your body into thinking that it is at home.
b. substitute "jet lag" for "circadian cycle."
c. be rested when you arrive.
d. not know the local time when you arrive.

**3.** If you break long trips with stopovers, you give your body time to
a. cycle.      b. adjust.      c. lag.      d. work.

**4.** Underline the sentences that imply that you should not plan much activity on your first day at your destination.

— Practice Exercise *19* —

Hunters may shoot their prey from quite a distance, but photographers find that the atmosphere deteriorates the image too much beyond a hundred yards—ninety meters or so. With a gun you need only put a single shot into your victim, but with a movie camera you may need four hundred pictures smoothly joined by a movement so perfect that those pictures will not jiggle or jump when they are projected—and every picture must be in sharp focus!

I think every nature photographer believes that some personal demon follows him or her about with the sole purpose of thwarting his or her every effort. When the sun is shining everything is quiet, but the moment it disappears behind a cloud the action starts. Put a big telephoto lens on your camera and an alligator catches a fish right under your nose.

1. From the main idea of the first paragraph, you can conclude that the author considers nature photography
   a. more difficult than hunting.
   b. financially rewarding.
   c. a profession haunted by demons and gremlins.
   d. always amusing.

2. Because the atmosphere deteriorates the image too much beyond a hundred yards, the photographer
   a. must get closer to the subject.
   b. needs a variety of expensive equipment.
   c. requires a sunny, unclouded sky.
   d. must use a large telephoto lens.

3. Because moving cameras must not jiggle or jump, you can conclude that the nature cinematographer must have
   a. a sharp eye.
   b. the largest telephoto lens.
   c. a vivid imagination.
   d. a steady hand.

4. Underline the sentence that suggests that it would be a good idea for a nature photographer to carry two cameras with lenses for closeups and distant shots.

— Practice Exercise **20** —

The scorpion is a fierce-looking creature with an armored, jointed body supported by eight legs. It has many eyes, yet for all practical purposes, it is almost blind. It feels its way around with large, fingerlike pincers. These pincers are powerful weapons with which the scorpion seizes and crushes its prey. The jointed tail, with its poisonous needle point, can be used with deadly accuracy in case the pincers are not effective. Sinister as they may be in the insect world, scorpions devour many varieties of insects that destroy grain fields. In one day, for example, an adult scorpion dines on nearly a hundred of these destructive insects. Though a person will find the pain from a scorpion's sting sharp, and the pain may last a few days, there is little danger of serious or lasting damage.

**1.** The author implies that people
   a. need not fear scorpions.
   b. should breed scorpions for crop protection.
   c. should kill scorpions outside grain fields.
   d. should consider keeping scorpions as pets.

**2.** You can conclude that, because the scorpion is almost blind, it
   a. is not aware of prey at a distance.
   b. moves with amazing speed.
   c. lashes out viciously with its needle-sharp tail.
   d. can inflict terrible damage on human beings.

**3.** The paragraph implies that the scorpion uses its poison
   a. whenever it is threatened.
   b. as a last resort.
   c. to provoke its enemies.
   d. only against people.

**4.** Underline the sentence that suggests that scorpions are useful to farmers.

# PART FIVE

## *Writing Activities*

The writing activities that follow will help you draw conclusions in writing. They will also help you apply that skill to your own writing.

Complete each activity carefully. Your teacher may ask you to work alone or may prefer to have you work with other students.

In many cases, you will be asked to write your answers on separate paper. Your teacher may ask you to write those answers in a notebook or journal so that all your writing activities will be in the same place.

Because the activities gradually increase in difficulty, you should review each completed activity before you begin a new one. Reread the lesson in Parts One and Two (pages 5–16) if you have any questions about drawing conclusions.

### *Writing Activity 1*

Read the following passage from "Innocents of Broadway"
by O. Henry.

"One summer me and Andy Tucker, my partner, went to
New York to lay in our annual assortment of clothes and
gents' furnishings. We was always pompous and regardless
dressers, finding that looks went further than anything else
in our business, except maybe our knowledge of railroad
schedules and an autograph photo of the President that
Loeb sent us, probably by mistake. Andy wrote a nature
letter once and sent it in about animals that he had seen
caught in a trap lots of times. Loeb must have read it
'triplets' instead of 'trap lots,' and sent the photo. Anyhow,
it was useful to us to show people as a guarantee of good
faith.

"Me and Andy never cared much to do business in New
York. It was too much like pot hunting. Catching suckers in
that town is like dynamiting a Texas lake for bass. All you
have to do anywhere between the North and East rivers is to
stand in the street with an open bag marked 'Drop packages
of money here. No checks or loose bills taken.' You have a
cop handy to club pikers who try to chip in post office
orders and Canadian money, and that's all there is to New
York for a hunter who loves his profession. So me and Andy
used to just nature fake the town. We'd get out our
spyglasses and watch the woodcocks along the Broadway
swamps putting plaster casts on their broken legs, and then
we'd sneak away without firing a shot."

A. Complete each sentence by drawing a logical conclusion. Your teacher may ask you to discuss your answers with the class.

1. You can conclude that the narrator feels that doing business with New Yorkers is

_____ .

2. The narrator says that he and his partner went to New York to "lay in their annual assortment of clothes and gents' furnishings." They went to New York to shop because

_____ .

3. The narrator compares himself and his partner to hunters. You might conclude that they could compare their customers to

_____ .

B. On a separate piece of paper or in your writing notebook, answer the following questions. Your teacher may ask you to work together with another student. Remember to refer back to the details in the passage when answering the questions.

4. Based on how the narrator views his customers, how do you think his customers react to him?

5. Why is the narrator reluctant to take checks or loose bills from his customers?

6. Why is a railroad schedule important to the narrator and his partner?

## *Writing Activity 2*

Read the following passage from *The Mysterious Island* by
Jules Verne. A group of Union prisoners escaping in a
hot-air balloon from the siege of Richmond struggle to
survive on an uncharted island.

---

The reporter [Spilett] hunted again in the pockets of his
trousers, waistcoat, and great-coat, and at last to Pencroft's
great joy, no less to his extreme surprise felt a tiny piece of
wood entangled in the lining of his waistcoat. He seized it
with his fingers through the stuff, but he could not get it
out. If this was a match and a single one, it was of great
importance not to rub off the phosphorous.

"Will you let me try?" said the boy, and very cleverly,
without breaking it, he managed to draw out the wretched
yet precious little bit of wood which was of such great
importance to these poor men. It was unused.

"Hurrah!" cried Pencroft. "It is as good as having a
whole cargo!" He took the match, and followed by his
companions, entered the cave.

This small piece of wood, of which so many in an
inhabited country are wasted with indifference, and are of
no value, must be used here with the greatest caution.

The sailor first made sure it was quite dry; that done, "We
must have some paper," he said.

"Here," replied Spilett, after some hesitation tearing a leaf
out of his notebook.

---

**A.**  On a separate piece of paper or in your writing notebook, answer the following questions. Refer back to the passage to check your answers. Your teacher may ask you to discuss your answers with the class.

**1.** You can conclude that the men are trying to build a fire. Why is a fire important to them?

**2.** Why was it of great importance not to rub the phosphorous off the match head?

**3.** Why was Spilett hesitant about offering a sheet of his notebook paper as tinder?

**B.**  Imagine that you are the leader of a group of people stranded on an unknown island. On a separate piece of paper or in your writing notebook, list some qualities that a courageous leader might have. How might a courageous leader use those qualities in a difficult situation?

Write a brief paragraph describing the courageous person. Use your list of ideas to help you. After you have finished your paragraph, ask another student to read it. What conclusions can the student draw about the person in your paragraph?

## *Writing Activity 3*

Read the following passage about sea lions.

Sea lions belong to a group of mammals called *pinnipeds*. The word *pinniped* comes from a Latin word that means "fin-footed." Sea lions are animals that have a sleek body with large, paddle-like flippers instead of legs. These flippers allow them to walk on land and move effortlessly through the water.

Sea lions spend much of their lives in cold water along the edges of continents and islands. Between its skin and muscles, a sea lion has a thick layer of fat called blubber that provides insulation from the cold. Sea lions are excellent divers because they store twice as much oxygen in their bodies as human beings. They also have large eyes and excellent night vision. Sea lions have whiskers on their upper lips that are sensitive to touch.

**A.** Complete each sentence by drawing a logical conclusion. Refer back to the passage to check your answers. Your teacher may ask you to discuss your answers with the class.

**1.** Because of its unique body structure, you can conclude that a sea lion

_____.

**2.** Based on information in the passage, you can conclude that sea lions live

_____.

**3.** Because sea lions can store more oxygen than other mammals, they can

_____.

**4.** You can conclude that the excellent night vision of a sea lion helps it

_____.

**5.** A sea lion can use its sensitive whiskers to

_____.

**B.** Choose an animal and write a paragraph using interesting facts about the animal. You may need to use reference books to find out specific details. Then write a question that asks the reader to draw a conclusion about your animal. Exchange your paragraph with a classmate. Read the paragraphs and answer each other's questions.

## Writing Activity 4

Read the following passage from "Mrs. Todd" by Sarah
Orne Jewett.

---

Later, there was only one fault to find with this choice of a
summer lodging-place, and that was its complete lack of
seclusion. At first the tiny house of Mrs. Almira Todd, which
stood with its end to the street, appeared to be retired and
sheltered enough from the busy world, behind its bushy bit
of a green garden, in which all the blooming things, two or
three gay hollyhocks and some London-pride, were pushed
back against the gray-shingled wall. It was a queer little
garden and puzzling to a stranger, the few flowers being put
at a disadvantage by so much greenery; but the discovery
was soon made that Mrs. Todd was an ardent lover of herbs,
both wild and tame, and the sea-breezes blew into the low
end-window of the house laden with not only sweet-brier
and sweet-mary, but balm and sage and borage and mint,
wormwood and southernwood. If Mrs. Todd had occasion
to step into the far corner of her herb plot, she trod heavily
upon thyme, and made its fragrant presence known with all
the rest. Being a very large person, her full skirts brushed
and bent almost every slender stalk that her feet missed. You
could always tell when she was stepping about there, even
when you were half awake in the morning, and learned to
know, in the course of a few weeks' experience, in exactly
which corner of the garden she might be.

**A.**    On a separate piece of paper or in your writing notebook, answer the following questions. Refer back to the passage to check your answers. Your teacher may ask you to discuss your answers with the class.

**1.** The passage says that Mrs. Todd has a very unusual garden. What caused people to think the garden was unusual?

**2.** People seemed to know where Mrs. Todd was. What caused them to know?

**3.** Beside stepping on the herbs, what else did Mrs. Todd do that caused the herbs to break?

**B.**    Imagine that you are Mrs. Todd's neighbor. How would you describe her? What things would cause you to think that way about her? On a separate piece of paper or in your writing notebook, list some of the things you know about Mrs. Todd.

Write a brief paragraph describing Mrs. Todd. Use your list of ideas to help you. After you have finished your paragraph, ask another student to read it. What conclusions can the student draw about Mrs. Todd based on your paragraph?

## *Writing Activity 5*

Read the following passage from "Rip Van Winkle" by
Washington Irving.

---

Whoever has made a voyage up the Hudson must
remember the Kaatskill Mountains. They are a dismembered
branch of the great Appalachian family, and are seen away to
the west of the river, swelling up to a noble height, and
lording it over the surrounding country. Every change of
season, every change of weather, indeed, every hour of the
day, produces some change in the magical hues and shapes
of these mountains, and they are regarded by all the good
wives, far and near, as perfect barometers. When the weather
is fair and settled, they are clothed in blue and purple, and
print their bold outlines on the clear evening sky; but
sometimes, when the rest of the landscape is cloudless, they
will gather a hood of gray vapors about their summits,
which, in the last rays of the setting sun, will flow and light
up like a crown of glory.

At the foot of these fairy mountains, the voyager may have
seen the light smoke curling up from a village, whose
shingle-roofs gleam among the trees, just where the blue
tints of the upland melt away into the fresh green of the
nearer landscape. It is a little village, of great antiquity,
having been founded by some of the Dutch colonists in the
early times of the province, just about the beginning of the
government of the good Peter Stuyvesant (may he rest in
peace!), and there were some of the houses of the original
settlers standing within a few years, built of small yellow
bricks brought from Holland, having latticed windows and
gable fronts, surmounted with weather-cocks.

---

**A.** On a separate piece of paper or in your writing notebook, answer the following questions. Refer back to the passage to check your answers. Your teacher may ask you to discuss your answers with the class.

**1.** What causes changes in the appearance of the mountains? Find several examples.

**2.** What causes the mountains to look various colors? Give examples of two colors from the text.

**3.** How do you think the author feels about the mountains? Draw a conclusion based on this passage.

**B.** Write a paragraph describing an unusual landform, monument, or statue in your area. Tell about it and include details that tell what you think about it. After you have finished writing, ask another student to read your paragraph. What conclusions did he or she draw about your feelings towards the object you chose?

## *Writing Activity* 6

**A.**  Carla heard the hurricane warning sirens. Her youngest son, Louis, was due home twenty minutes ago.

On a separate piece of paper or in your writing notebook, describe what happens to Carla and Louis. If Carla hears hurricane warning sirens, where does she live? Why is Louis late? What can you conclude about Carla's feelings? Your paragraph should lead a reader to a reasonable conclusion.

**B.**  Ask another student to read your paragraph and have him or her draw a conclusion. Do you agree with the conclusion? Is the conclusion logical? What in your writing helped the student draw that conclusion? Your teacher may want you to share the results with the class.

# ANSWER KEY

## Practice Exercise 1

1. d          2. a          3. d
4. Paper with a high "rag content"—that is, paper made literally from rags or from fibers more like flax and hemp—is not subject to the same decaying process.

## Practice Exercise 2

1. c          2. a          3. c
4. She then looks for standing water in which to lay her eggs—a pond, a pool, a swamp, or even a pail of rainwater.

## Practice Exercise 3

1. d          2. b          3. c
4. When they molt they are unable to fly.

## Practice Exercise 4

1. a          2. b          3. c
4. Absences have been halved.

## Practice Exercise 5

1. c          2. a          3. a
4. In a recent year, more than eight million bikes were sold in the United States, and a third of them went to adults. The year before, only 15 percent of new bike sales were for adults.

## Practice Exercise 6

1. d          2. b          3. a
4. Thousands of feet above, astonished airline pilots saw Manhattan fade, then disappear.

## Practice Exercise 7

1. b          2. a          3. d
4. It can be tamed and taught to perform complicated tricks, even to mimic human speech.

## Practice Exercise 8

1. c          2. d          3. d
4. Unfortunately, narrow lanes mean less room for drivers to correct their mistakes or inattention, and less room for the swaying of a car in a crosswind. Two cars on narrow lanes may actually touch even though the tires will be within their respective lanes.

## Practice Exercise 9

1. a          2. b          3. d
4. We aren't educated to reusing resources, or even recognizing the value of "waste" products.

## Practice Exercise 10

1. b          2. a          3. d
4. Pharmacies, moreover, are seldom heavily staffed.

## Practice Exercise 11

1. c          2. c          3. a
4. A purebred dog is a type of dog that is recognized by the American Kennel Club as a distinct breed.

## Practice Exercise 12

1. b          2. d          3. d
4. This large piston presses the sheet of metal against the die that shapes it.

## Practice Exercise 13

1. a          3. c          3. d
4. Edward F. Carpenter, headmaster of "The Prep," as it is known by the students, admits that it isn't easy.

## Practice Exercise 14

1. c        2. a        3. b
4. In its own low-key self-promotion, Boston neither brags of its past nor projects some galactic future.

## Practice Exercise 15

1. b        2. d        3. d
4. Studies have shown that most injuries and deaths resulting from accidents are caused when people are thrown out of or against the interior of the vehicle.

## Practice Exercise 16

1. c        2. a        3. d
4. Treating our waste water *before* it is discharged into lakes, rivers, or the ocean is far less expensive.

## Practice Exercise 17

1. c        2. b        3. b
4. Thanks to the Egyptian climate, we know more about the vanished Egyptians than we know about any other ancient people, much more than we know about the early Greeks and Romans, whose civilizations died just yesterday.

## Practice Exercise 18

1. a        2. c        3. b
4. Upon arrival, take it easy. Don't try to adjust to local time schedules all at once.

## Practice Exercise 19

1. a        2. a        3. d
4. Put a big telephoto lens on your camera and an alligator catches a fish right under your nose.

## Practice Exercise 20

1. a        2. a        3. b
4. Sinister as they may be in the insect world, scorpions devour many varieties of insects that destroy grain fields.

# PROGRESS CHART

| Practice Exercise Number | Put an X through the number of each question answered correctly. | | | | Total Number Correct |
|---|---|---|---|---|---|
| | Question | Question | Question | Question | |
| 1 | 1 | 2 | 3 | 4 | |
| 2 | 1 | 2 | 3 | 4 | |
| 3 | 1 | 2 | 3 | 4 | |
| 4 | 1 | 2 | 3 | 4 | |
| 5 | 1 | 2 | 3 | 4 | |
| 6 | 1 | 2 | 3 | 4 | |
| 7 | 1 | 2 | 3 | 4 | |
| 8 | 1 | 2 | 3 | 4 | |
| 9 | 1 | 2 | 3 | 4 | |
| 10 | 1 | 2 | 3 | 4 | |
| 11 | 1 | 2 | 3 | 4 | |
| 12 | 1 | 2 | 3 | 4 | |
| 13 | 1 | 2 | 3 | 4 | |
| 14 | 1 | 2 | 3 | 4 | |
| 15 | 1 | 2 | 3 | 4 | |
| 16 | 1 | 2 | 3 | 4 | |
| 17 | 1 | 2 | 3 | 4 | |
| 18 | 1 | 2 | 3 | 4 | |
| 19 | 1 | 2 | 3 | 4 | |
| 20 | 1 | 2 | 3 | 4 | |

**Total of correct answers for all 20 exercises:**

Rating:  70–80  Excellent
55–69  Good
40–54  Fair